Intro by editor

Great Manager Institute™ was built from the ground up with nothing but a vision. Dreamers and thinkers alike joined forces to foresee a world where every individual got the opportunity to work with a Great People Manager™.

Being the offspring of a company whose vision is to make the world a Great Place to Work®, Great Manager Institute™ looks a bit further to identify the real agents of creating great workplaces. Employees are guided and mentored by their managers, managers who lie at the heart of any workplace culture.

What came first – Great Organizations and Great Managers?

Trusting in the latter, we identified the immediate need for a school of thought that assesses and nurtures managers as the link between employees and their organization. Partnering with data and futuristic technological trends, this vision grew to become what it is today.

The Great People Manager™ Study was launched to give managers and organizations a manner to capture quantitative and qualitative feedback from their employees. This helps to gauge the People Manager Effectiveness Index© in a step towards becoming Great People Manager™s and Companies with Great People Manager™s.

Driven by a passion for unconventional and non-traditional ideas, Rashmi Mutt leads the Branding and Communication Team. #ManagerMantras is her brainchild, now being spread across the world of managers.

Preface

Dear Managers,

Isn't it fascinating to play the role that you do? Delivering results by managing a set of people and processes, boundaries and bosses, expectations and uncertainties – being a manager is at once a joy and challenge. Never is there a day that goes without its share of novelty!

To add to this esoteric mix of fun is the fact that there is no clear guideline as to how to develop into the role of a manager. Expectations from the role keep changing, and so does your own perspective. You come across so many other managers around you and keep learning from each of them – sometimes the right things, sometimes the wrong ones. But becoming a great manager is a never-ending process – you never stop learning.

Considering so many variables that affect your behavior and your performance, isn't it natural for you to wonder what makes some managers stand out as 'great'?

While we agree that there is no 'one' answer to that question, we have learned that like medicine, management is largely a 'practice'. The more you do – the better you get at it.

The challenge is to get ideas about how to improve your practice. How to deal with those tricky situations where you could not come up with a 'solution'. You look around, but do not see anyone doing any better. You hesitate to ask others because you are not sure whether it will be appreciated.

This short book is our effort to help you out. Here we have collected a set of 'mantras' about practices that some of the great managers have adopted in the domain of people management – the most intriguing aspect of your role! While your context may be different, you will still be inspired to try some of these in your own way.

To make it easy, we have grouped these practices into three categories – Connect, Inspire, and Develop.

When you read these stories you will be able to empathize with the managers and live their experiences – as if you see them in action. We are confident that these stories will not only be a great reading but will also take you further on your journey to become a 'great' manager. Hence the name, Manager Mantras.

Dive into it and discover your own Mantra!

- Anantadeb Bandyopadhyay

CONNECT

"I conduct one-on-one meetings with team members to address performance and individual issues they may be facing. We also collectively address team issues, stemming from a lack of bonding being observed. By organizing activities for them to interact with each other, the gap was bridged and the rapport among the team strengthened"

"*Every month, we have a workmen communication session. This helps to share important information regarding customer complaints, quality issues and actions for improvement. This helps for top management information to reach team members on a regular basis.*"

"In individual meetings with team members, we discuss both professional and personal matters. They share practices implemented in their previous companies to get an idea of how to achieve cost-saving. We discuss their family and life goals, which helps to build a better connect."

"As a part of our customer service newsletter, a Case Study was shared with the team. This helped to bring about more awareness and learning, leading to overall development. Everyone shared their feedback post this, building a more collaborative environment."

"Of late, I've decided to focus more on Listening and less on Speaking. The team felt good being able to share their opinions openly in an informal manner. Through this practice, we've moved beyond the traditional setting of a group meeting, enabling real-time feedback."

"By conducting regular one-to-one meetings with the team, I'm able to build a strong connect with each member. I listen to their concerns and ideas which need focus, based on which we create individual development plans for the next few months. All plans are uploaded for everyone to see, so that there is transparency and visibility."

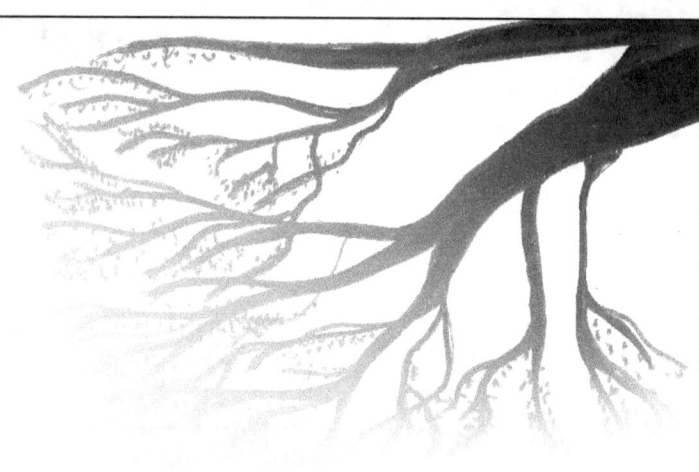

"*Through our daily technical discussions, each person can share their technical knowledge with the entire team. This has led to an increase in technical competency in such a short timeframe. Thanks to this, we can easily collaborate on new projects by using our shared knowledge.*"

"*I initiated a practice called TAG-it, where I acknowledge each team member's contribution to ensure that the whole team is aware. I have begun sharing individual strengths and a feedback email with each team member. This has led to increased respect and thankfulness towards one another.*"

"We arrange a dinner for the entire team at an off-site location once a month. This relaxes them and reduces any formalities so that they can share their needs and expectations with one another."

"On the 1st Friday of every month, the team gathers after work hours for a team-bonding session. Through informal discussions, each member shares their ideas for team improvement. This improves the relationship and team spirit within the entire team."

"As the team works across locations, there is no forum to discuss concerns and challenges. Due to this, we started a monthly Team ki Adalat for the team to come together to ask questions. I also try to share the latest information and resolve any issue."

"We started the Best Buddy Chain - a chain format of working for the team members. As a result of this, everyone ensured collaboration and took pride in its successful implementation. This created an environment for everyone to give their personal best."

"We created a team web portal to serve as a listening forum. Each team member can ask any question, which is further liked or answered by other team members. The most liked question is answered in a Skype Session or Webinar Forum conducted monthly."

"We get all the team members on one common platform for a face-to-face discussion, regardless of their location. We plan these meetings as video conferences to build a connect and understanding among all members."

"Every first Thursday of the month, we host a platform for all associates to speak about their challenges and how to tackle them. This is called 'Voice of Associates', to let them talk about things bothering them and come up with solutions to the same."

DEVELOP

"*Every Monday, the team spends an hour discussing projects updates and policy changes that may affect the current work. Team members bring forth innovative solutions to tackle existing or possible challenges. We collectively discuss concepts for process improvements and test feasibility by bouncing ideas off one another.*"

"We planned a session for all team members to share knowledge on project-related matters. We started a buddy program to give each member exposure and hands-on training, giving them confidence to handle bigger projects. This helps to improve technical skills and thought process of each individual, making them valuable assets."

"My team members weren't being able to complete their projects on time. We initiated a monthly review to explore new ideas. By offering each other suggestions for improving performance, the learning of the team was enhanced. This created a healthy sense of competition among them as well."

"Our team created a maintenance server for storing everything as a soft copy. From then onwards, everybody could access any information through this document and all communication would reach everyone. By working on the same sheet, the need for more documentation was reduced."

"We conduct departmental meetings to discuss issues and solutions without interrupted communication. On a rotation basis, different team members are responsible for conducting the meetings. This helps to receive updates and identify pain areas within a stipulated time frame."

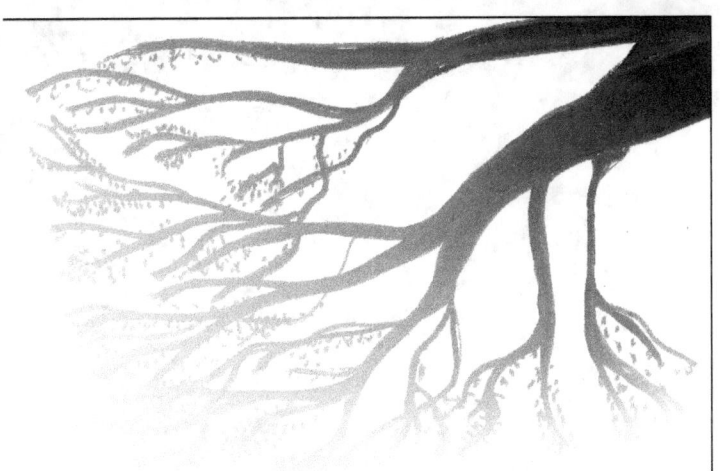

"Every Tuesday, I spend time in training my team members to help them perform better. Together, we create Individual Development Plans, and see to it that respective needs are being met. This has now become a routine part of our responsibilities."

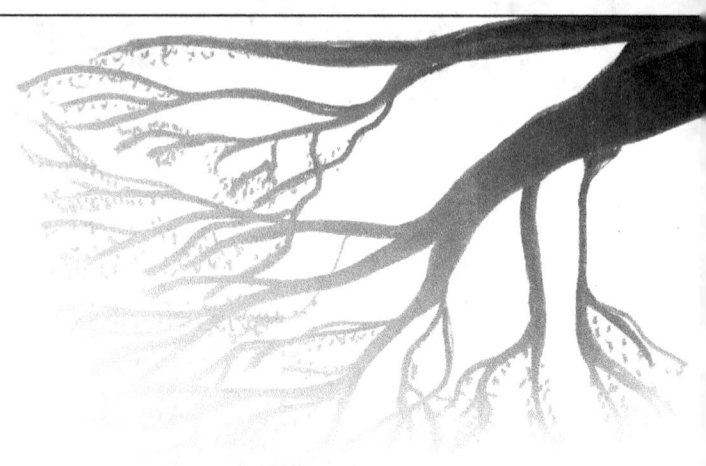

"During appraisal time, each team member is mapped to another to conduct a SWOT analysis for them. This helps to share individualized views and learn quickly, as compared to classroom-type of learning. Team members in turn felt more empowered and developed through this practice."

"All stakeholders related to the project execution, including the client, sit together to discuss project progress. All problems and reasons for the delay are shared such that solutions can be reached. These progress meetings are held every 2 weeks."

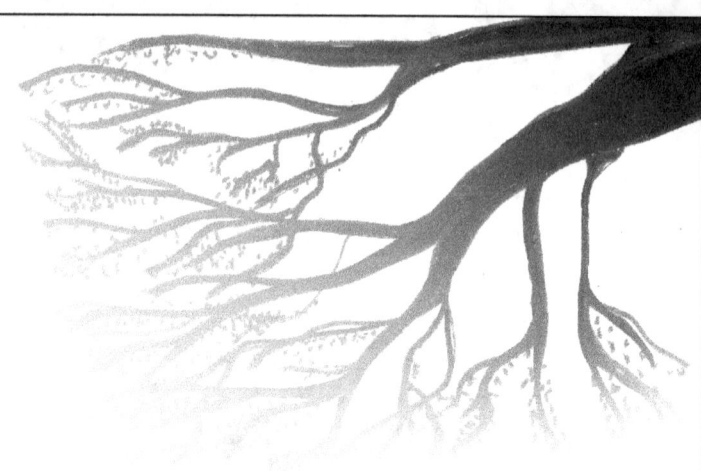

"*Each team member discussed their career aspirations and development plans with me. Based on these discussions, we created a task list and responsibility sheet for them to meet their goals. The aim is to enable team members to move up in their careers fruitfully.*"

"We created a platform to share innovative ideas and provide an opportunity to be implemented. This was done to develop the engineering ability of all team members. Everyone seems excited as unconventional ideas have already begun flowing in."

"To unify the team, we encourage team members to have personal interactions. Through a Test Box, the team can build an environment to trade skills and practice with each other. They then do research on more efficient methods to use for projects."

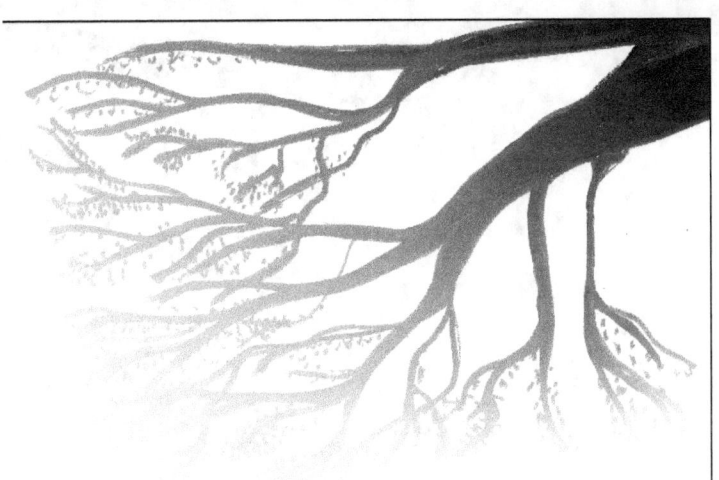

"*Associates can choose any technology they prefer for a project with the aim to cross-skill themselves. This shouldn't affect current progress, but associates can ask for permission to practice. This helps them focus on their self-development.*"

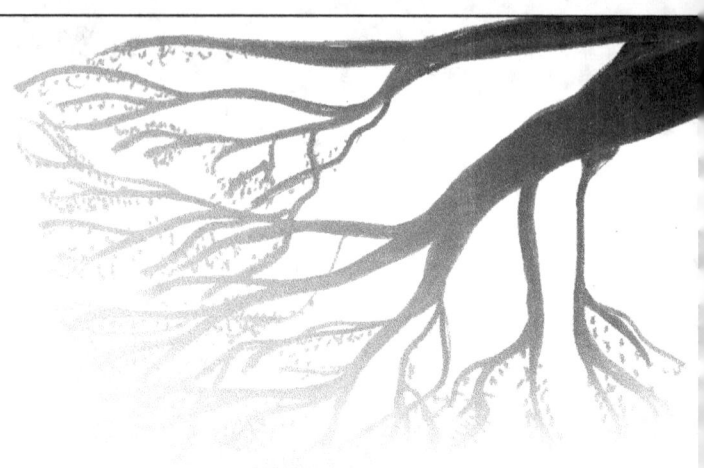

"We developed a Skill Matrix for each member, based on which we created Competency Development plans. We revise these plans on a half-yearly basis. We identified key technological topics for team members to deepen their knowledge."

"*Every morning, we hold a team huddle for 15 minutes to discuss project progress. A guest speaker comes to speak about a pre-decided technical topic. A learning roundtable is held to speak about topics that the team has recently gained knowledge on.*"

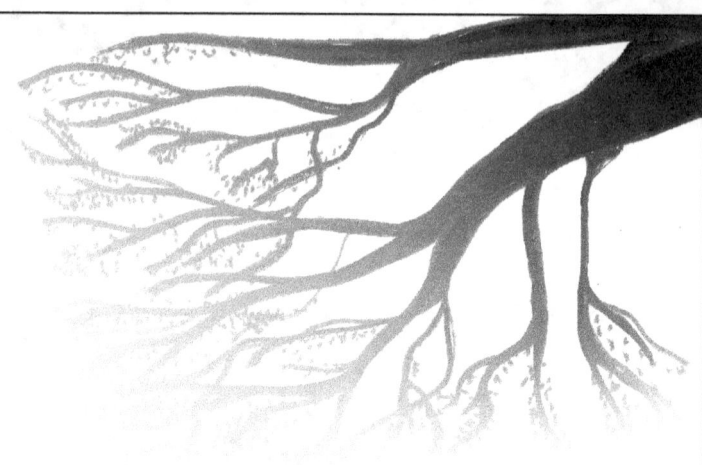

"Unique Ted-style sessions are held to develop interest beyond one's comfort zone. This has helped to identify areas of innovation and grow the scope of work. One session helped us to identify potential leaders for a leadership training program."

INSPIRE

"*Each team member has a daily target, which if achieved, is responded to with spot applause and their favorite chocolate. This data is tracked week-wise for Recognition activity that takes place on each floor. This has not only inculcated a healthy sense of competition among team members, but productivity has grown as a result.*"

"We had an issue with a client where did they not agree with our methodology. The team collaborated to figure out why there was a gap in the current process, which led to them realizing that post-lunch sessions resulted in errors due to drowsiness. They implemented a 20-minute post-lunch Laughter Club to remove the monotony and keep the quality of the product intact."

"We conduct 'Family Day', where everyone leaves office by 6:30 pm. This has helped team members to spend quality time with their families and also improve efficiency of their jobs. By conducting this regularly, it has become a strong part of our work culture."

"*On any day of the month, each team member is allowed to leave office 2 hours early. This can be availed based on their personal choice and requirements. The team has seen an improvement in performance as a result of this.*"

"At the end of every month, we conduct a thanking practice titled Euphoria. This serves as a platform for people to share their gratitude towards others and for everyone to be aware of individual contributions. We also celebrate birthdays and milestone achievements to build an atmosphere of fun."

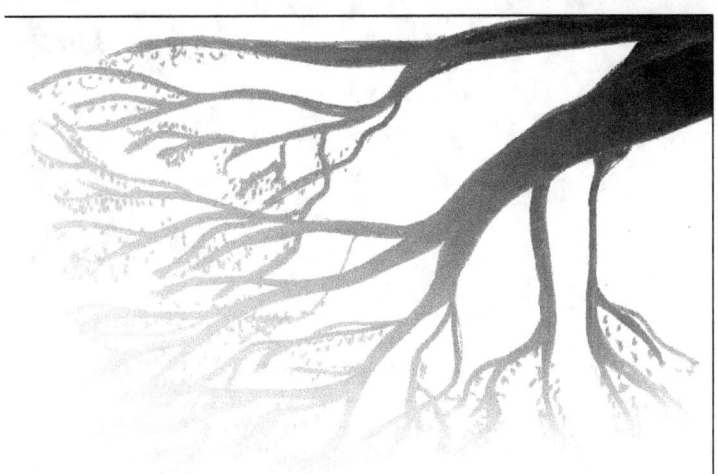

"We started an applause portal to thank team members personally. A widespread feeling of recognition has overcome the whole team. We also implemented the Tech Genius Award for contributions to product enhancements and guidance for other functionalities."

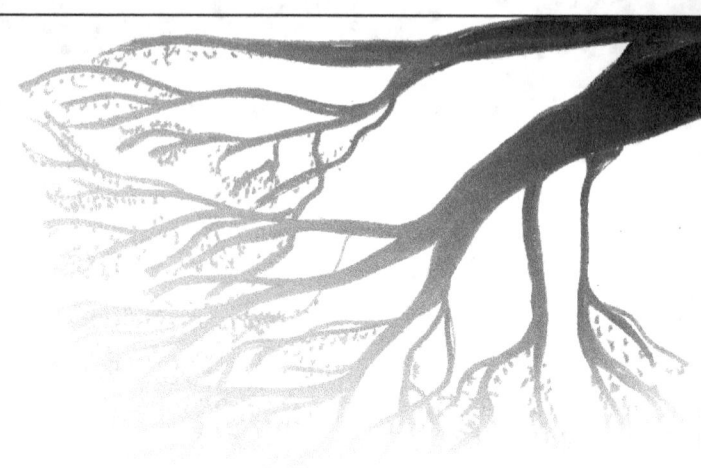

"*Each team member is asked to share an inspiring story related to their personal experiences. This could be any story that has added some meaning to their life. Others listen and add their comments at the end of each sharing session.*"

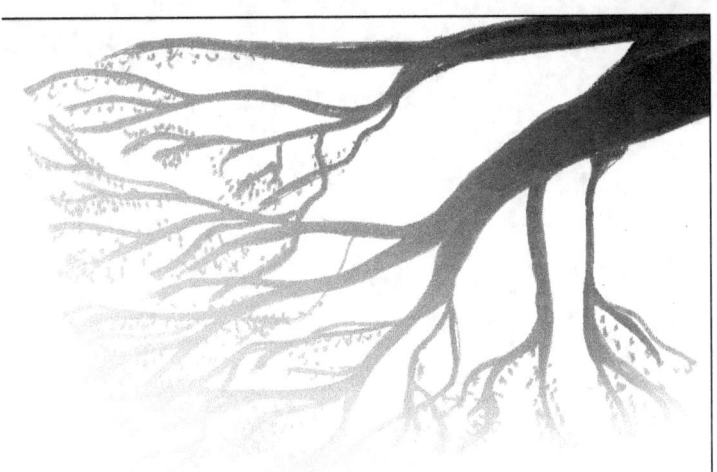

"Before starting any project, we conduct a Brief Time session which is attended by all the workers at the project site. We cover factory-related matters, like safety and installation. This reduces the anxiety they may have before starting a project."

"The Star of the Month program was started to thank peers for their contributions. In stand-up meetings, they openly thank each other for good work and award a star to them. The individual with the highest stars at the end of the month wins the award."

"We set up a tree with photos of each team member attached. To thank each other, they pin a smiley badge or rosebud along with a note specifying why the appreciation. This practice has helped the team become grateful towards each other."

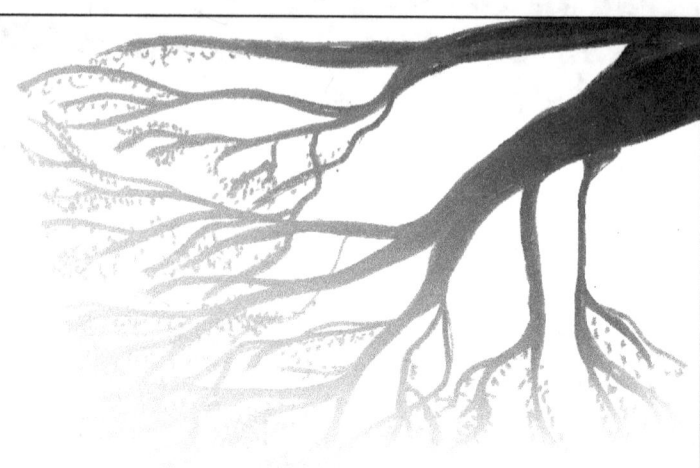

"In our team's intranet, we have a portal named Birthday Bash with details of each member's birthday and is used to convey wishes also. Appreciation is also passed through here, and those with the highest number receive a gift from the Department Head."

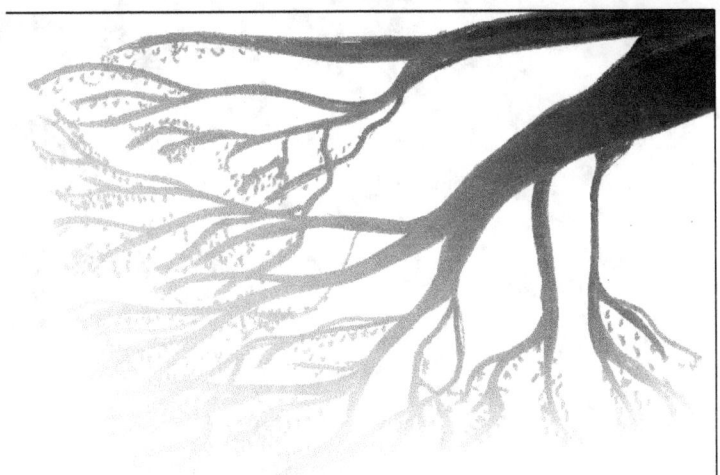

"We planned a team lunch to bring in positivity and motivation among all team members. We used this opportunity to thank and share good moments with each other. We conducted fun games and team building activities also to improve the team bonding."

"My team members began publishing blogs on our intranet with their individual viewpoints. This started receiving appreciation from other teams as a means of motivating each other. Through this visibility, they felt more inspired to talk about their work."

"One of our team members is physically challenged and was having trouble finding a new job. The team came together to support her in the job-seeking process. This strengthened the unity and team feeling, and helped us show her that we care."

"Our monthly thanking activity has brought in a great amount of team spirit. Each member puts a chit into the Thanking Box to appreciate someone. At the end of the month, the member with the highest number of appreciations is adjudged the 'Masterpiece'."

"On our team intranet, each member can post his achievement along with a nomination. Team members can then vote against each nomination. The most voted team member is named the 'Team Super Hero'. The team then sponsors a movie ticket for the superhero."

"Once a week, we hold 'Early Wednesday' where a chit is picked and the team member chosen gets to go home at 4 pm. Now everyone looks forward to Wednesdays and utilizing their extra time effectively."

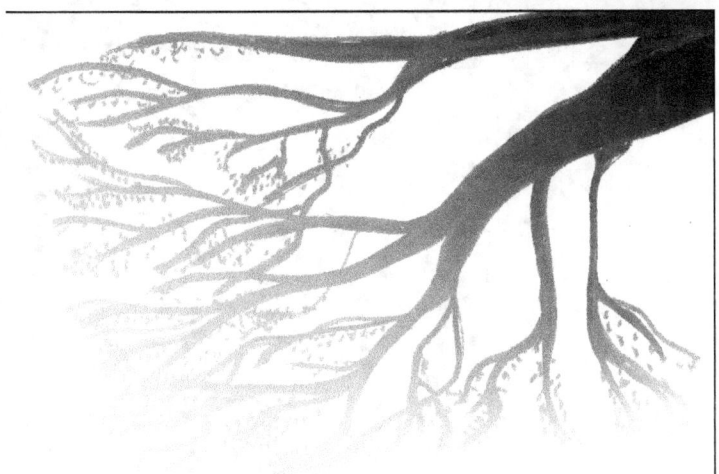

"Our practice 'Helping Hands' is a display mechanism which carries various notes of appreciation. During our meetings, team members can post notes to thank people for supporting them. This had built in a culture of appreciation and recognition."

"We have made an Excel-based application for conducting our recognition. We made 2 categories for appreciations – one for project tasks and one for general contributions. We share a report each month to highlight these appreciations with the whole team."

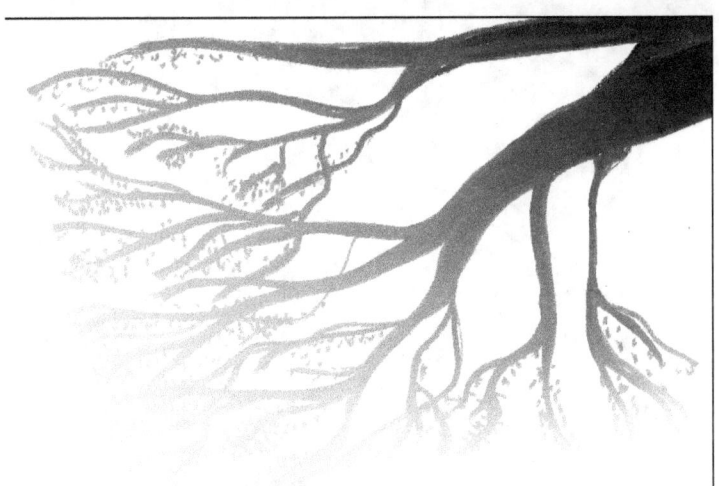

"A box is kept in a common area for team members to vote for their 'Shining Star' of the month. At the end of the month, the votes are counted and the winner is rewarded accordingly. The entire team eats lunch together to build team spirit among them."